Life of Bailey

Learning Is Fun Series:

Alphabet ABC'S

Sensei Paul David

COPYRIGHT PAGE

Life of Bailey - Learning Is Fun Series: Alphabet ABC'S

by Sensei Paul David,

Copyright © 2023

All rights reserved

978-1-77848-286-1 LifeOfBailey_Learning_ABCs_Amazon_PaperbackBook

978-1-77848-285-4 LifeOfBailey_Learning_ABCs_Amazon_eBook

978-1-77848-410-0 LifeOfBailey_Learning_ABCs_Ingram_PaperbackBook

This book is not authorized for free distribution copying.

www.senseipublishing.com

@senseipublishing
#senseipublishing

Get Our FREE Books Now!

lifeofbailey.senseipublishing.com

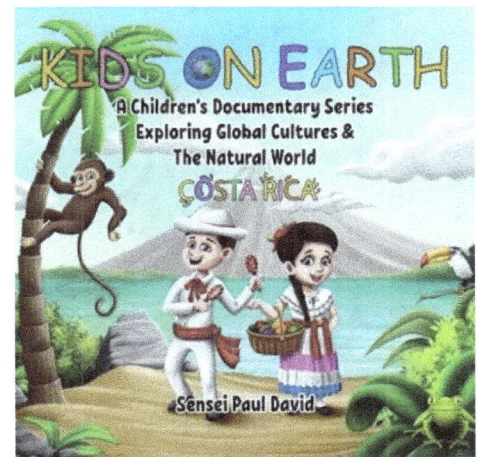

kidsonearth.senseipublishing.com

Click Below or Search Amazon for Another Book In Each Series Or Visit:

www.amazon.com/author/senseipauldavid

 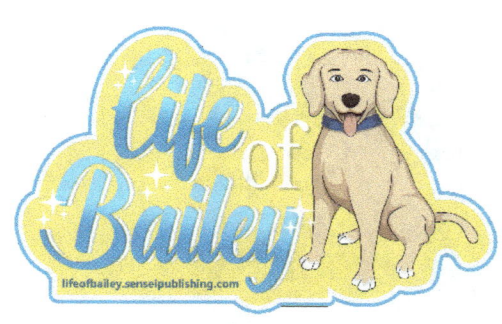

Join Our Publishing Journey!

If you would like to receive FUTURE FREE BOOKS and get to know us better, please click www.senseipublishing.com and join our newsletter by entering your email address in the pop-up box.

Follow Our Blog: senseipauldavid.ca

Follow/Like/Subscribe: Facebook, Instagram, YouTube: @senseipublishing

Scan the QR Code with your phone or tablet to follow us on social media:

Like / Subscribe / Follow

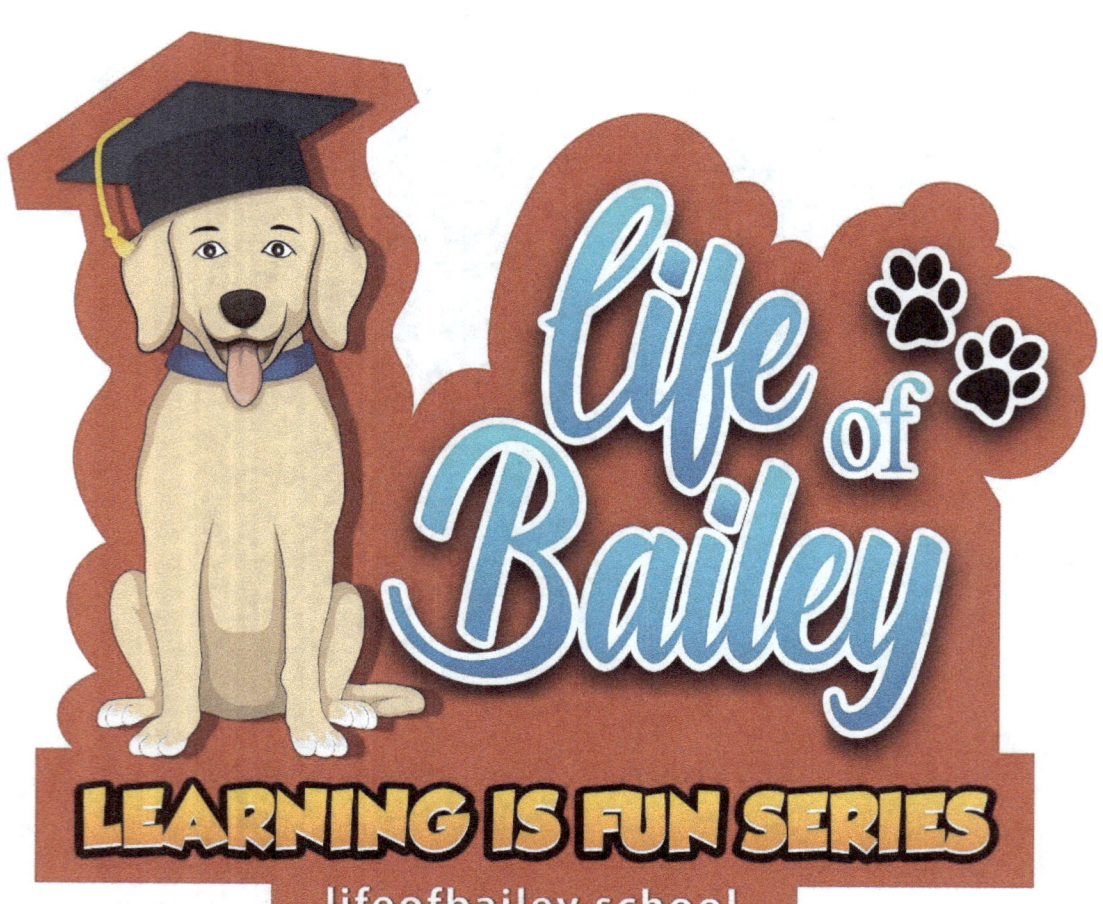

Synopsis: Bailey the Dog takes kids on an exciting journey as he introduces each letter of the alphabet. Bailey shows kids how the alphabet is used in everyday life by providing interesting examples for each letter. He also provides fun examples that help kids remember and practice the alphabet. Along the way, Bailey's enthusiasm and curiosity show kids how much fun learning can be.

Introduction: Hello young readers! I'm Bailey, the friendly neighborhood pup. I'm here to teach you the alphabet and what each letter stands for. I'm sure you'll have lots of fun learning with me! Let's get started!

A is for... Apple - I love to eat apples when I can find them! How many apples do you see?

B is for… Bear – I'm happy to sleep beside my teddy bear. Do you have a teddy bear too?

C is for... Cat - I can't wait to watch cats explore and play from my back yard. How do you spell cat? C - A - T!

D is for... Duck - I like to watch the ducks swim in the pond. Sometimes I wish I could swim like a duck and stay dry on water. Would you like to learn to swim someday?

E is for... Elephant - Yesterday I said hello to the elephants in the zoo with my Daddy. Have you been to the zoo?

F is for... Fish – If I'm quiet and still I can see the fish swim in the stream. Would you like to see how fish swim up close?

G is for... Giraffe – One time I saw the giraffes in the savannah. They have long necks and are very calm.

H is for... Horse - I love to watch the horses run in the field. They look like big dogs to me. How many horses do you see?

I is for... Ice Cream – One time my mommy let me lick her ice cream when it was hot outside. It tasted very sweet and felt very cold. Do you like ice cream too?

J is for... Jellyfish – One time I watched a jellyfish move in the ocean on TV with my Daddy. I thought it was food at first but now I know that jelly fish are alive like you and me.

K is for... Kite – I'm curious to watch the kites fly in the sky. I wish I could fly too. What do you think it would feel like to fly like a kite?

L is for... Lion – My daddy once dressed me up as a lion for Halloween. I tried to roar like a lion in the jungle. Can you roar too?

M is for... Monkey - I love to watch the howler monkeys swing in the trees in Costa Rica. They are very loud.

N is for... Nest - I love to watch birds make nests in their tree homes. Can you imagine living in a nest so high up a tree? Wow!

O is for... Owl – I can see the owls hoot at night. They look very serious. Can you put on a serious face like an owl?

P is for... Pig – I laughed when I saw pigs play in the mud. Do you know what color the pigs are?

Q is for... Queen - I love to watch the queen butterflies flutter in the garden. Have you ever seen a butterfly before?

R is for... Rabbit – I like to try and hop like the rabbits in the yard. Can you hop like a bunny rabbit?

S is for... Star - I really like to watch the stars twinkle in the night sky. Did you know the stars in the sky are like our sun? - Just very far away!

T is for... Tiger – I saw a tiger in the zoo with my Daddy. I tried to say hello, but the tiger fell asleep. Do you know when your bedtime is?

U is for... Umbrella – I saw my Grandma's umbrella open up in the rain. It made a funny popping sound. Do you know what rain sounds like? Can you try to make the sound of rain?

V is for... Violin – I heard violin music in the park with my Daddy. We sat down and listened. Did you know a violin is made from a tree?

W is for… Whale – On a big boat with my parents, I saw a whale jump out of the ocean. This wale is called an Orca. Can you name the colors of the Orca whale?

X is for... X-Ray – My Daddy took me to the animal hospital once, and the doctor showed us a picture of my bones. The doctor used an X-Ray machine to take the picture. Can you imagine what your bones look like in your body?

Y is for... Yellow – My Grandma's favorite color is yellow. Sometimes I see her eating a yellow banana in the backyard, but I would rather have an apple. What's your favorite color?

Z is for... Zebra - I love to watch the zebras run in the grass. Zebras are from a country called Africa. Can you say "Africa?"

Help us color in this picture of Bailey. Share your creative artwork on Facebook and Instagram by tagging @lifeofbailey

Follow/Like/Subscribe/Share on Facebook, Instagram, @lifeofbailey

YouTube & Google Search: #senseipublishing

Thank you for reading this book!

If you found this book helpful, I would be grateful if you would **post an honest review on Amazon** so this book can reach other supportive readers like you!

All you need to do is digitally flip to the back and leave your review. Or visit amazon.com/author/senseipauldavid click the correct book cover and click on the blue link next to the yellow stars that say, "customer reviews."

As always…

It's a great day to be alive!

Get/Share Our FREE All-Ages Mental Health Books Now!

lifeofbailey.senseipublishing.com

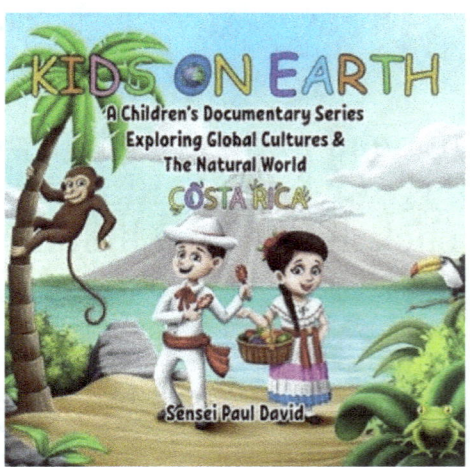

kidsonearth.senseipublishing.com

Click Below or Search Amazon for Another Book In Each Series Or Visit:

www.amazon.com/author/senseipauldavid

Check out our **recommendations** for other books for adults & kids plus other great resources by visiting
www.senseipublishing.com/resources/

Join Our Publishing Journey!

If you would like to receive FREE BOOKS, special offers, please visit www.senseipublishing.com and join our newsletter by entering your email address in the pop-up box

Follow Our Engaging Blog NOW! senseipauldavid.ca

Get Our FREE Books Today!

Click & Share the Links Below

FREE Kids Books

lifeofbailey.senseipublishing.com
kidsonearth.senseipublishing.com

FREE Self-Development Book

senseiselfdevelopment.senseipublishing.com

FREE BONUS!!!
Experience Over 25 FREE Engaging Guided Meditations!

Prized Skills & Practices for Adults & Kids. Help Restore Deep Sleep, Lower Stress, Improve Posture, Navigate Uncertainty & More.

Download the Free Insight Timer App and click the link below:
http://insig.ht/sensei_paul

About Sensei Publishing

Sensei Publishing commits itself to helping people of all ages transform into better versions of themselves by providing high-quality and research-based self-development books with an emphasis on mental health and guided meditations. Sensei Publishing offers well-written e-books, audiobooks, paperbacks and online courses that simplify complicated but practical topics in line with its mission to inspire people towards positive transformation.

It's a great day to be alive!

About the Author

I create simple & transformative eBooks & Guided Meditations for Adults & Children proven to help navigate uncertainty, solve niche problems & bring families closer together.

I'm a former finance project manager, private pilot, jiu-jitsu instructor, musician & former University of Toronto Fitness Trainer. I prefer a science-based approach to focus on these & other areas in my life to stay humble & hungry to evolve. I hope you enjoy my work and I'd love to hear your feedback.

- It's a great day to be alive!
Sensei Paul David

Scan & Follow/Like/Subscribe: Facebook, Instagram, YouTube: @senseipublishing

Scan using your phone/iPad camera for Social Media
Visit us at www.senseipublishing.com and sign up for our newsletter to learn more about our exciting books and to experience our FREE Guided Meditations for Kids & Adults.

www.ingramcontent.com/pod-product-compliance
Lightning Source LLC
Chambersburg PA
CBHW080023110526
44587CB00021BA/3747